Newbridge Discovery Links®

Artists at Work

Marilee Burton

W9-BEL-965

Newbridge

A Haights Cross Communications Company

Artists at Work
ISBN: 1-58273-707-X

Program Author: Dr. Brenda Parkes, Literacy Expert
Teacher Reviewer: Kerri Blaus, Sleepy Hollow Elementary School, Sleepy Hollow, IL

Written by Marilee Burton

Newbridge Educational Publishing
333 East 38th Street, New York, NY 10016
www.newbridgeonline.com

Copyright © 2002 Newbridge Educational Publishing,
a Haights Cross Communications Company

Cover Photograph: Artist painting a white clay mask
Table of Contents Photograph: Leaping gazelles from *The Lion King*

Photo Credits
Cover: Roberto Soncin Gerometta/Photo 20-20/Picturequest; Table of Contents page: Joan Marcus;
page 4: Sanders & Mock/Photofest; page 5: (top) Rod Rolle/Liaison, (bottom) Kenneth Van Sickle/Courtesy
of Oberlin College; page 6: Tom and Dee Ann McCarthy/CorbisStockMarket; page 7: Jacqueline Lissy, (inset)
AFP/CORBIS; page 8: Joan Marcus; page 9: Charles and Josette Lenars/CORBIS; page 10: Joan Marcus;
page 11: (left) Joan Marcus, (right) Richard Drew/AP/WideWorld Photos; page 12: Andre Jenny/Focus
Group/Picturequest; page 13: Bettmann/CORBIS; page 14: Peter Yates/Courtesy of the University of
Michigan; page 15: Cheri Smith; page 16: Dave Martin/AP/Wide World Photos, (inset) Jay Sailors/AP/
WideWorld Photos; page 17: Richard Howard/Black Star Publishing/Picturequest; page 18: Lynn Goldsmith/
CORBIS; page 19: Nubar Alexanian/CORBIS; page 20: Bettmann/CORBIS; page 21: CORBIS, EyeWire;
page 22: Greg Gibson/AP/WideWorld Photos

10 9 8 7 6 5 4 3 2

TABLE OF CONTENTS

INTRODUCTION

Have you ever listened to a band playing and started to tap your toes to the beat of the music?

Have you ever laughed or cried while watching a movie or a play?

Have you ever looked at a painting or **sculpture** that really excited you?

Maya Lin
sculptor and architect

Wynton Marsalis (right)
musician and composer

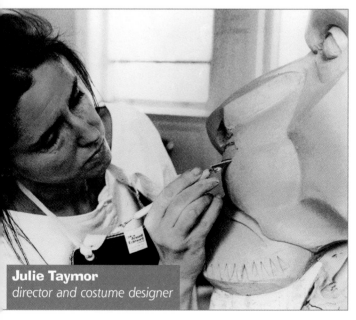

Julie Taymor
director and costume designer

If you answered yes to any of these questions, an artist was talking to you!

Artists speak to us in many ways. When you see or hear their work and feel something inside, you are listening to what they have to say.

But it's not always easy to create beautiful music or a wonderful play. It takes imagination to become an artist. And lots of time and practice, too.

This is the story of three very different kinds of artists. Yet they all use their imagination. And they all work hard to share their ideas with others . . . and with you!

JULIE TAYMOR: Creating Magic Onstage

Butterflies! That's what Julie Taymor feels inside as she waits for the curtain to rise.

The theater is filled with people eager to see the play *The Lion King*. Julie is the **director** of the play and the costume designer. She worked for two years to create this **musical**. Now it's time to tell the story onstage in front of an audience.

"Will they like the show?" Julie wonders. It won't be long before she finds out.

Disney's *The Lion King* was first created as an animated movie. Julie Taymor helped turn the film into a live show.

These Singing Apples are from *The Green Bird*, a play that Julie directed as a grown-up. She also designed the masks and puppets for the play.

Julie's interest in the theater began when she was seven years old. Growing up in Newton, Massachusetts, she and her older sister put on shows in their backyard.

But Julie didn't just act in the plays. She made the scenery and props as well. It was fun for her to imagine new worlds and bring them to life.

By the time she was ten, Julie was taking acting lessons. The training sparked her imagination. In one class, she was asked to pretend to be "frightened with your toes"!

Julie traveled to other countries to study. And wherever she went, she learned new things about the theater. At 16, she went to Paris to study **mime**. This form of acting taught her how to tell stories through body movement instead of words.

After college, Julie went to Indonesia to learn about shadow puppets and mask-making. She was fascinated by the way the puppeteers used light and shadow to help tell a story.

Shadow-puppet shows have been performed in Indonesia for thousands of years. The puppeteer holds the shadow puppet behind a white sheet. Rods attached to the puppet are used to make it move.

Julie returned to the United States full of excitement and new ideas. She had learned so much to help her create magical worlds onstage. As a director and costume designer, Julie could use all of it.

With *The Lion King*, she did just that. Sleek cheetahs, proud lionesses, and other animals of Africa come to life in unusual costumes that look like great big puppets.

The curtain begins to rise for the opening of *The Lion King*. A brightly colored baboon begins to chant. Two lanky giraffes stroll across the stage. A huge elephant shuffles down the aisle of the theater.

Soon the audience is clapping and cheering. Julie Taymor has brought the African plain to life in the imagination of her audience. The show is a success!

Julie designs her animal costumes so they don't completely hide the actors who wear them. That way, the people in the audience can use their imagination to help create the characters.

Julie won Tony Awards for directing *The Lion King* and for designing the costumes.

MAYA LIN: Blending Art with Nature

Maya Lin wasn't surprised when she heard that she had won a contest to design the Vietnam Veterans **Memorial**. She wasn't surprised because she didn't believe it!

Maya never expected to win. She was only 21. She was a college student. And she had only entered the contest as an assignment for an **architecture** class. But Maya's design won.

The Vietnam Veterans Memorial in Washington, D.C., seems to grow out of the earth. The memorial honors Americans who died in the Vietnam War. Each name is carved into the wall.

Maya Lin holds a model of her winning design. Maya's design was chosen out of 1,421 entries.

Maya grew up surrounded by art and books. Her father taught art and made ceramics. Her mother taught literature and wrote poetry. They encouraged Maya and her older brother to explore the arts as well.

Maya was a good student. Her favorite subjects were math and science. She also loved working with her hands. After school, she would make little buildings and sculptures out of clay or paper scraps.

But Maya liked to spend time outdoors, too, exploring the rocks, streams, and hills around her home in Athens, Ohio. Nature was important to her.

In college, Maya found a way to combine art, math, and science with nature—architecture!

As an artist, she could imagine beautiful structures. With math and science she could solve design puzzles, such as how tall or wide something should be.

Maya often starts her plans with an artist's **model** that she makes by hand. Her very first model for the Vietnam Veterans Memorial was made in the college dining hall with mashed potatoes!

Maya designs things that blend in with the earth. Sometimes she even creates sculptures out of the earth itself. These are known as **earthworks**.

One of her most famous earthworks is called *Wave Field*. Maya made this for the engineering building at the University of Michigan in Ann Arbor. For this project, Maya learned about aerodynamics, which involve air and motion. Aerodynamics made her think of rolling ocean waves.

In *Wave Field*, the curves of the waves are just the right size for students to curl up in and read a book.

Maya Lin often starts a project by thinking about what its purpose will be. Next she learns about the project and visits the site where it will be built. After that, her imagination goes to work and she comes up with an idea. For many artists, it takes a long time for an idea to take shape. Maya's friends say she "lays an egg" because her ideas come to her almost fully formed.

That's how Maya created the Civil Rights Memorial in Montgomery, Alabama. This monument honors people who died in the fight for equal rights.

Events in civil rights history are carved into the memorial. Water flows over it to help visitors reflect on the past.

Maya Lin's drafting table is filled with tools and blueprints, or plans, for new projects.

Today, Maya has her own design firm in New York City. She tries to make nature a part of everything she creates.

In 1999, she designed the Langston Hughes Library in Clinton, Tennessee. The library stands in a grassy field, peacefully surrounded by trees with a pond nearby.

Maya Lin hopes that people who view her work will feel a connection to the earth. As she says, "Maybe I'm just asking you to pay closer attention to the land."

WYNTON MARSALIS: Making Great Music

"**G**ood evening, ladies and gentlemen. Thank you for coming out this evening. We hope you enjoy yourselves. Because we are here to swing."

This is the way Wynton Marsalis, one of the greatest trumpet players in the world, begins his concerts. Standing onstage with the other jazz musicians in his group, Wynton then raises his trumpet to his lips. And he begins to blow!

Every year Wynton travels all over the world to give concerts. He has performed in more than 30 countries on six different continents.

One of the things Wynton Marsalis likes to do when he's not playing music is write it. He also selects the music for his concerts.

Wynton grew up in a musical family. His father played piano, and four of his five brothers played instruments, too.

Wynton wasn't always a great musician. The first time he played the trumpet, he said it sounded "sad." He felt that the trumpet honked and brayed. And he didn't practice, so he didn't get better.

His feelings changed when he joined his high school band. To prove himself to his teacher, he began to practice his trumpet—every single day.

"I would listen to trumpet players all the time," Wynton says. "I just fell in love with playing."

He kept on practicing. He didn't miss a day of practice for seven years in order to achieve his goal.

And achieve it he did! After high school, Wynton won a music scholarship. Before long, he was invited to join a jazz band. Soon he started his own band. By age 22, Wynton Marsalis was performing all over the country, making records, and winning awards.

After performing at the Grammy Awards in 1984, Wynton took home two awards himself—one for jazz and one for classical music.

Jazz musicians use several different wind instruments. They call them "horns."

trumpet

saxophone

trombone

clarinet

Playing music makes Wynton feel good. "When I play the trumpet," he says, "all my troubles disappear." And the music he loves most is **jazz**. This kind of music was first played by African Americans more than 100 years ago. It has lots of **rhythm** and swing.

Wynton also likes teaching people about jazz— especially children. He wants everyone to enjoy this special kind of American music.

Wynton spends time teaching kids because he wants to help them all love music as much as he does.

Wynton Marsalis has many jobs. He plays trumpet. He conducts orchestras. He **composes** music. And he teaches children about music.

Wynton visits schools and listens to children play music. He always gives young musicians the same advice: "All you have to do is practice. Then all of that braying, honking, and spraying becomes playing."

GLOSSARY

architecture: the art of designing buildings

compose: to write music

director: the person who supervises the actors and staging of a show

earthwork: a work of art that is made by reshaping the land in an artistic way

jazz: a kind of music in which the musicians often invent new ways to play tunes as they go along

memorial: something that is built or made that helps people remember a person or event

mime: a form of acting in which body movement instead of words is used to tell the story

model: a small-sized copy of a building or monument that is made before the actual structure is built

musical: a play or film that features singing and dancing

rhythm: a regular pattern of sounds in music; the beat

sculpture: a work of art that is shaped out of wood, clay, metal, or other materials

INDEX

WEBSITES

To learn more about these artists, log on to

www.google.com/search?q=julie+taymor
music.acu.edu/www/iawm/pages/lin/lin.html
www.trumpetjazz.com

You'll find some cool art activities at this site:
www.arts.ufl.edu/art/rt_room/index.html